MUSEUM GUIDES FOR

Kids

Impressionist Art

Ruthie Knapp and Janice Lehmberg

Davis Publications, Inc.
Worcester, Massachusetts

Hello! I'm your tour guide, Rembrandt. This is a painting I did of myself. I have done lots of portraits of myself—about 100, in fact. In 1629 I finished this painting called *Artist in His Studio*. And *I'm* the artist, Rembrandt.

I've spent almost four hundred years trying to finish the painting on the easel. Do I ever need a break!

I am going to hang up my palette with the one you see behind me on the wall and unlatch the door to your right. Then I can join you from time to time as you read this book. I would like to help you look at Impressionist art. After all, three centuries of painting have taught me a trick or two!

Rembrandt van Rijn, *Artist in His Studio*, 1629.

© 1998 Janice G. Lehmberg and Ruth C. Knapp
Illustrations © John McIntosh of McIntosh Ink, Inc.

Printed in Italy
Library of Congress No. 98-60875
ISBN: 0-87192-385-8
10 9 8 7 6 5 4 3 2 1

Front cover: Pierre-Auguste Renoir, *Luncheon of the Boating Party*, 1881. The Phillips Collection, Washington, DC.

A contribution from the proceeds of the sale of this book will be donated to The Sally Leahy Scholarship Fund. Scholarships are awarded to children from the Greater Boston area for art classes held at the Museum of Fine Arts.

Contents

Introduction

Museum is a word like eggplant. It doesn't appeal to everyone. Have you ever gone to a museum in hopes of a great experience? It sounds easy enough: centuries of culture will speak to you from age-darkened canvases, sculptures, and small coins. History will come clear. Well, if history doesn't come clear, at least you'll be surrounded by many beautiful old things. Wrong!

Museum The word *museum* comes from the Greek word, *mouseion*. It means "a temple to the Muses." In Greek mythology, Zeus, king of the Greek gods, had nine beautiful daughters who never grew old. They were called the Muses and inspired creativity. Ancient Greek artists and writers asked the Muses to inspire them before they started work. We hope that you will look to a museum for inspiration, too!

Welcome to museum feet.

Museum feet is that tired feeling you get after spending too much time in a museum. A case of museum feet makes you feel like saying: "This is boring. I could have done that myself. That's ugly. I'm hungry. I'm really hot. When can we sit down? What time is it?"

Studies of museum behavior show that the average visitor spends four seconds looking at an object. Children are more interested in smells, sounds, the "feel" of a place, and other people's faces than they are in looking at a work of art. Adults, sometimes unfamiliar with what they are seeing, cannot always answer children's questions. After a museum visit, it is only a short time before almost everything is forgotten. Within a family or group of five, no one member will remember a shared museum experience the same way.

We have written this book to help people of all ages enjoy new ways of looking at works of art, ways that make looking memorable and fun. Come with us and learn how to banish the **boring** and feature the **fun.**

Why do museums show so much old stuff? Not all museums collect old things. There are hundreds of kinds of museums in the United States. They range from a nut museum and a Mack truck museum to the largest thermometer museum in the world. There is even a Museum of Bad Art!

Use your flashlight

Common questions

A good idea

A   Closer Look

Look closely at museum objects

Did You Know...

Additional information

Avoiding Museum Feet

To avoid museum feet, try not to look at too many things. Studies show that young visitors get more out of a visit if they focus on seven (plus or minus two) objects—either five or nine objects. The fewer objects you see, the more you'll remember. One and a half hours is the ideal time to keep your eyes and mind sharp, and your feet happy!

Making personal connections with museum objects helps to form lasting memories. If you are looking at a French Impressionist painting, you might relate to the artist by thinking, "I'll bet the Impressionists had fun painting everything around them. But it must have been hard knowing that many people were going to make fun of the way they were painting."

Remember to take your time when looking at art.

"You can enjoy a work of art for as long as it takes to smell an orange. Then, to keep your interest, you have to do something more."
—SIR KENNETH CLARK,
BRITISH ART HISTORIAN, 1903–1983

This book is about doing something more.

What to bring
✓ Paper and pencil with eraser
✓ Sit-on-the-floor clothes
✓ A plan of action
✓ A small flashlight
✓ A snack for the ride

Finding Your Way

A museum may feel big and confusing when you first arrive. If you are not familiar with the museum, find the Information Center or a guard. Ask for directions to the collection you want to see. Pick up a map with a floor plan of the museum.

Rooms in a museum are called **galleries.** Museums aren't the only places that have galleries. Prairie dogs, moles, and ants live in underground galleries. Old ships had galleries, and so did forts.

Labels

Every work of art in a museum has a label. In a French collection, a label might look like this:

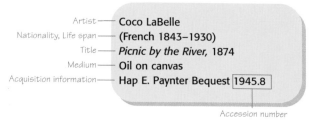

Artist —— Coco LaBelle
Nationality, Life span —— (French 1843–1930)
Title —— *Picnic by the River,* 1874
Medium —— Oil on canvas
Acquisition information —— Hap E. Paynter Bequest 1945.8

Accession number

Let's look at the label above. Coco LaBelle was the artist. She was French and lived from 1843 until 1930. The title of the painting is *Picnic by the River.* Coco painted it with oil on canvas in 1874 when she was thirty-one years old. Hap E. Paynter left this painting to the museum in his will.

Accession numbers The accession number on the label is 1945.8, which means the museum received it in 1945, and it was the eighth object to be collected that year. You sometimes see small red numbers painted on the back and sides of small objects in a museum. These are also accession numbers.

Instruments or thingamabobs in museum galleries and cases Some visitors are as interested in conservation equipment as they are in the objects on display. The *hygrometer* is a small dial that measures the humidity inside a display case. The *hygrothermograph* is a larger device that records the temperature and humidity of a museum gallery. These are often seen on the floor in a corner of the gallery.

Your Turn to Smell the Orange

Form your first impression of the work of art. Choose an object. Let your eyes wander all over the surface. Absorb it. It is special, and it is yours. Taking time to look at a work of art is important because there is always more to it than first meets the eye.

Study this drawing carefully. What is it? Ask someone else what he or she thinks it is. Once you have taken a long look at a work of art, turn away from it. Wait a few seconds, and turn back to look at it again. What is new this time?

When you are taking your first look at French Impressionist paintings, don't stand too close to them. They look better from a distance.

Look at the Three Distances

When you look at a painting, think of three distances. The **foreground** is the part closest to you. In *Bougival*, it shows a dirt road. The **middleground** is the area *between* what is closest to you and farthest away. Notice how blue the water is there. The **background** is the part that is farthest away. This painting shows buildings and trees against a dappled sky. Train yourself to look first at the foreground, then into the middle, and finally, deep into the painting. Looking at a painting this way helps you see things you would otherwise miss!

Alfred Sisley, *Bougival*, 1876.

 Why can't we touch things? Fingers contain oils and salts, which damage fragile museum objects. Have you ever seen the mark your fingerprint leaves on the blackboard?

Look at Color

Colors can make us feel a certain way. There are warm and cool colors. Warm colors are reds, oranges, and yellows. They make us think of fire. Restaurant owners often use red in their decor because it can make people hungry. Cool colors are blues, greens, and violets. These colors make us think of glaciers and ice. Blue paint is sometimes used for rooms in hot climates because it looks cool and fresh.

Some colors get pushy in paintings. They like to show off. These colors stand out in a painting and grab your attention. They are usually warm colors like red. But white also can stand out, especially against a dull color. Other colors are quiet. In a painting, these are the darker colors.

Think about what different colors mean to you. Is yellow a cheerful color? Does it make you think of sunshine or a sizzling egg, sunny-side up? Vincent van Gogh, the Post Impressionist, said that for him yellow was the color of love.

Where do paint colors come from? In the past, painters used colors, known as pigments, found in bugs, plants, sea creatures, rocks, earth, and metals. Have you ever gotten raspberry stains on your fingers or tiger lily pollen on your nose? These are colors found in nature, and they can be used to make dyes. These days, most paints are chemically colored.

Impressed by Color Bright colors are one of the hallmarks of French Impressionism. Many of the Impressionists painted outside, so they needed to use bright colors to capture natural light. Additionally, paint tubes with a wide choice of new colors had become available to artists. The Impressionists were also influenced by scientific studies that explained how color affects the eye.

Did You Know... One of Renoir's surviving paint palettes shows that some of the colors he used were white, cobalt blue, emerald green, crimson, Naples yellow, ultramarine blue, and vermillion (brilliant red).

Pierre-Auguste Renoir, *Woman with a Parasol and a Small Child on a Sunlit Hillside*. Renoir painted this scene of Camille Monet, wife of his good friend, Claude Monet.

A Closer Look

In this painting by Renoir, which color did you notice first? How many colors are there in the painting? Which color jumps out? Which is shy? Is one hot? cold? quiet? noisy? Is one color the king or the boss of the painting?

Jacques Henri Lartigue, *Cousin Caro and Mr. Plantevigne, Villerville*, 1906. Jacques Henri Lartigue was only twelve years old when he took this photograph of people using parasols at the beach. He went on to become a famous photographer.

Parasols

Parasols are a feature found in many Impressionist paintings. They were the fashion for women (and sometimes men), who were starting to spend more time outside. The word comes from the Latin words *parare*, "to shield," and *sol*, "sun."

- Look for parasols in Impressionist painting.
- What colors are reflected on the inside of the parasol?

Primary Colors

The three primary colors are **red, yellow,** and **blue.** All colors, except white and black, can be mixed from the three primary colors. But primary colors cannot be mixed from any other colors on earth.

Do you see the three primary colors—red, yellow, and blue—in *Vase of Flowers* by Dutch painter Jan van Huysum? Did you notice that several leaves and stems look blue instead of green? After two hundred and seventy years, the yellow pigment, which the artist mixed with blue pigment to make a green leaf tone, has faded from the light, leaving only the blue part of the color mixture. When pigments fade, they are called *fugitive* colors.

Jan van Huysum, *Vase of Flowers,* circa 1720.

Painting with Pasta?

When an artist uses very thick paint on a canvas, it is called *impasto.* An easy way to remember this word is to think of pasta. Then think about strips of fettuccine or linguine, like thick brushstrokes, lying across a plate. French Impressionist Claude Monet often used an impasto technique. So did van Gogh.

Complementary Colors

Each primary color has a "best friend" color, called a complementary color. The best friend color makes red look redder, blue look bluer, and yellow look more yellow. To find the complement, or best friend, of a primary color, mix the other two primary colors together. Red's best friend is **green** (yellow + blue). Blue's best friend is **orange** (yellow + red). Yellow's best friend is **violet** (blue + red).

Complementary Colors in Nature

Some complementary colors occur naturally outside. Think of clay flowerpots full of violet and yellow pansies, or red apples on green trees. Or blue butterflies with orange markings, and blue crocuses with orange centers. What about the blue embers of an orange flame?

Which complementary colors make up the little tree frog?
(**answer:** red and green)

Complementary Colors in Art

Can you find all three primary colors and their complements in *Woman Seated in a Chair* by Pablo Picasso? (**answer:** red and green walls; blue dress and orange floor; yellow and violet chair)

A   Closer Look

Pablo Picasso, *Woman Seated in a Chair*, 1941.

Edouard Manet, *Boating,* 1874.

Black and White

Scientists don't call black and white true colors. But imagine what paintings would look like without them. Artists use black to tone colors down and white to lighten them. Certain artists are famous for their use of black and white. John Singer Sargent, the American Impressionist, was admired for his handling of white; Edouard Manet, the French nineteenth-century artist, made striking use of black and white.

A   Closer Look

In *Boating,* the black ribbon on the woman's white hat draws your attention towards her face. The white form of the man allows him to stand out against the blue water.

One of Nature's Bugs

Renoir called black "one of nature's illnesses." Many of the French Impressionists used black sparingly.

Look at Shapes

Shapes, like colors, can send messages to viewers. The French Impressionists were primarily concerned with how shape was *defined* by color and light. Their shapes were created with dashes or strokes of paint. There was no outline to hold the color inside the form. Even sharp or pointed forms were made with dots and dabs of color. The triangular shapes of Monet's *Haystacks* (page 47) may have been used as a symbol of power. Haystacks represented agricultural wealth in the French countryside.

Look at *Bal à Bougival* by French Impressionist Pierre-Auguste Renoir. Using an imaginary magic finger, erase the red bonnet surrounding the dancing woman's face. What shape did you make? Erase the color in the yellow straw hat of her dancing partner. Did you make a circle? Continue to find circular shapes and curves in the foreground. You will find them in the outline of the dancers' shoes, the hem of her skirt, his trouser bottoms, and the bouquet of violets. Check the background. You will notice circular faces and hats as well as circular patterns in clothing. These repeated circular shapes lend an easygoing, happy feeling to the painting, echoed in the movement of the whirling dancers themselves.

Pierre-Auguste Renoir, *Bal à Bougival*. The dancing girl was Suzanne Valadon, one of Renoir's favorite models. She had once been a trapeze artist and tightrope walker in the circus.

Look at Line

Lines may be diagonal, curved, vertical, or horizontal. Diagonal lines are action lines. Curved lines give a sense of motion, too. A vertical line is a strong, stable line. It gives a feeling of balance. A horizontal line is a quiet line.

Paul Cézanne, *Mont Sainte Victoire*, circa 1897.

A Closer Look

When you look at *Mont Sainte Victoire* by Post Impressionist Paul Cézanne, think about the different kinds of lines in the painting. How do the diagonal lines of the tree on the right give it a sense of movement?

Strokes of Genius?

While many Impressionists sketched ideas in notebooks, most painted directly on canvas with no underdrawing. They used many small strokes of paint instead of lines to convey light and atmosphere.

Word Wizard

Horizontal The word *horizontal* comes from *horizon*, the seemingly flat line where the earth meets the sky.

Look at Composition

The way an artist arranges the color, line, and shape of a painting until it is just right is called *composition*. When you decorate a birthday cake or doodle on a frosty windowpane, you are making a composition. Artists plan their compositions to guide our eyes on a journey through their paintings.

Now think about the composition of *Mont Sainte Victoire*. Imagine how the painting might have looked if Cézanne had left out the trees in the foreground. What if he had left out the mountain? Every element of this painting is vital to the composition.

Look at Perspective

Artists use perspective to make a flat surface look as if it has depth. Look for tricks that artists use to create a sense of three-dimensional space on a two-dimensional surface:

- Artists make background objects smaller and less detailed because the eye sees less from a distance.
- Artists make background colors lighter as it fades into space because the sky appears lighter as it gets further away.
- Artists make parallel lines, like the sides of roads, come together to create deeper space.

The next time you are in a car, bus, train, or subway, notice the road or tracks in front of you. Notice how they come together as you follow them into the distance.

A **Closer Look**

Moroccan road.

The French Perspective

Lighter background colors create perspective in French Impressionist paintings. French Impressionists, however, were more interested in painting the effects of light than in creating deep space. Some of the Impressionists experimented with perspective. They adopted the perspectives they had seen in Japanese woodblock prints. Instead of showing a scene straight-on, they painted it as if they were looking down on it—a bird's-eye viewpoint. Or they showed only part of a scene, cutting someone off by a door frame or wall. Edgar Degas, Mary Cassatt, and Vincent van Gogh all tried out these new perspectives in their work.

"Lunatics" at Large

> Happy are those who see beauty
> in modest spots where others
> see nothing.
> CAMILLE PISSARRO

French Impressionist paintings are the rage in museums these days. Their light-splashed canvases draw crowds of viewers. But in the nineteenth century, they were the subject of ridicule. Pregnant women were warned that looking at them might be bad for their health! The Impressionists were called lunatics. One journalist wrote that after seeing the first Impressionist exhibition, a visitor started biting everyone in sight.

Policeman: "Lady, it would be unwise to enter!"

Art Oops!

One famous Post-Impressionist painting was used to stuff a hole in a chicken coop. Today it is in the Pushkin Museum in Moscow. Read on to see whose painting it was.

Why did people laugh at the paintings? When the Impressionists were painting, people were familiar with only one kind of art. It was called *Academic* painting (page 19). Compared to Academic painting, Impressionism looked messy and unfinished.

Who were the Impressionists? They were a group of serious artists who wanted to paint the people and places around them in a new way. Close in age, they became friends at art schools in Paris. Many of them painted outdoors together and shared ideas at cafés. The group was drawn together by their frustration with the French art establishment, which usually rejected their paintings from the Salon, the major art exhibition held in Paris. To find an audience for their art, the Impressionists arranged their own shows. These exhibitions gave them a group identity.

Impressionism and the Café Connection

A café was a kind of club where one could eat, drink, read the newspaper, and catch up on local gossip. Begun in the 1700s, after coffee was introduced into Europe, there were 30,000 cafés in Paris by 1870. Cafés were a popular theme in Impressionist painting.

A Closer Look

How many people are in this café sketch? Look in your gallery for a scene with the same number of people.

Edouard Manet, *A Café Interior,* 1869.

Café Guerbois It has been said that Impressionism began at Café Guerbois, seen in *A Café Interior.* For several years, it was the Impressionists' favorite café. They met to talk under its gaslights at the end of most days and regularly on Thursdays. Monet remembered that "nothing could have been more interesting than the discussions we had....They kept our wits sharpened, encouraged us to press ahead with our own experiments."

Word Wizard

Coffee Did you think the word *coffee* came from the French word *café?* In fact, it comes from Caffa, a region in Ethiopia to which coffee plants are native. Legend says that shepherds noticed their goats stayed awake all night after munching the leaves of the coffee plant.

The Impressionists and the Academic painters did not see eye-to-eye on much of anything!

What did the Impressionists paint? They painted everyday life and landscapes: their cities and villages, friends and pastimes. Where Academic artists painted angels, goddesses, and kings, the Impressionists portrayed haystacks, cafés, and train stations. These commonplace subjects challenged the rules of traditional French art.

What was the Impressionist style? Each Impressionist had his or her own style and approach. Most used bright colors and short brushstrokes to show the changing effects of natural light. Many, but not all, Impressionists painted outdoors. Unlike the Academic painters, the Impressionists did not make preliminary sketches before starting to paint. They painted directly on the canvas to record their sensations quickly. Breezy brushstrokes lent spontaneity to their work.

Why do Impressionist paintings look blurry? The Impressionists painted scenes filled with light and atmosphere. They did not want to "freeze" their subject matter by drawing hard outlines. They wanted natural light to shape them. New scientific studies had found that natural light was made up of many colors. The little brushstrokes of different colors, which the Impressionists used to form objects, act like light. They make the canvas shimmer. This is why their paintings look blurry!

A Closer Look When you are looking at Impressionist paintings, adjust to the viewing distance that's right for you. Don't stand too close. Move back and forth until it feels right.

Claude Monet, *Impression: Sunrise,* 1872. Monet said that he couldn't think of a title for this painting of Le Havre so he just wrote "Impression."

Did You Know...

The term **Impressionism** came out of the first Impressionist Exhibition in 1874. The title of Claude Monet's painting *Impression: Sunrise* inspired an art critic to call the style *Impressionism*.

What was Academic art? Academic art met the standards of the French Académie des Beaux-Arts. The Academy was made up of a group of artists who sponsored the annual art Salon and set guidelines about how artists should paint. Members of the Academy believed that classical Greek and Roman art was the perfect art and that artists should copy it. Artists were urged to paint important historical events, classical myths, and biblical scenes in a traditional manner.

Academic works had titles such as *Moses and the Ten Commandments* and *The Death of Caesar.* The canvas surfaces of Academic painting were satiny smooth; you couldn't tell where one brushstroke ended and another began. Details were precisely drawn and every degree of light and shade was used to model objects. The human figure was as flawless as a classical sculpture.

William Bouguereau, *Homer and His Guide*, 1874.
This painting of the blind poet who wrote The
Iliad was made the same year as the first
Impressionist Exhibition in which Monet's
Impression: Sunrise was seen.

• Compare Monet's *Impression: Sunrise* (page 19) with Bouguereau's *Homer and His Guide*. How are they different?

• Find an Academic painting in your museum that shows a historical, biblical, or mythical scene. Study it so you can compare it to a French Impressionist painting. Some other French academic artists are Jacques-Louis David and Jean-Léon Gérôme.

How did Academic art start? In the past, churches and kings were the main patrons of art, so artists painted subjects that would appeal to their tastes. Battles, heroes, biblical scenes, and myths became routine. Most Academic paintings were very large because they were made to hang in palaces, churches, and state buildings.

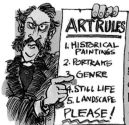

Art Rules For two centuries, the French Academy had rated the subjects that artists painted. Historical paintings, including religious and mythological scenes, were deemed best. Portraits were rated second best. Genre painting, still lifes, and landscapes were third best, in that order.

• Look for two examples of the five subjects that were rated by the French Academy.

A Closer Look

• Which type of painting do you like best?

Winslow Homer, *Art Students and Copyists in the Louvre Gallery, Paris,* 1868. Artists had to get a permit to copy paintings at the Louvre.

Copycats First

L'Ecole des Beaux-Arts (School of Fine Arts) in Paris was the most famous art school in the Western world. Its teaching was supervised by the French Academy. French art education stressed drawing the human body. Art students learned by copying engravings, plaster casts, and finally, live models. Copying the Old Masters at the Louvre was also part of an artist's education. Degas advised, "One must copy and copy the masters before one has the right to do a radish from nature."

Atelier Most of the Impressionists studied at ateliers. Monet, Renoir, and Sisley met at Gleyre's atelier. An *atelier* was a small art studio, usually run by a professor from L'Ecole des Beaux-Arts. The "master" teacher came by twice a week to instruct students.

Felicien Myrbach-Rheinfeld, *Candidates for Admission to the Paris Salon*, circa 1885. Some of the 4,000 entries to the Paris Art Salon.

Impressionist Enemy # 1: The Salon Named after the Salon Carré (square room) in the Louvre, the Salon d'Art was the annual, state-sponsored art exhibition in Paris. A two-hundred-year tradition, the Salon was the cultural event of the year. Up to 4,000 works of art were chosen by jury to be on view for two months. Every artist hoped his or her work would be in the show where it could be seen by dealers, collectors, and critics. The problem for the Impressionists was getting in! The Salon jury was mostly made up of Ecole des Beaux-Arts professors, who favored Academic painting.

The Salon jury dismissed paintings with the ease of a broom sweeping away unwanted dust.

Stamped R for Reject

Rejected Salon paintings were returned with a large **R** stamped on the back of the canvas. An artist had to re-line the canvas to hide the **R** if she or he wanted to sell the painting. No one wanted to buy a painting that had been refused by the Salon!

Skyed at the Salon? Artists who the jury liked were hung "on the line," or at eye level. Artists whose works were considered inferior were "skyed," or hung high above eye level where their paintings were hard to see.

Word Wizard

Vernissage The opening preview of the Salon was called the *vernissage*. This name came from the coat of varnish (*vernis* in French) that artists applied to their paintings just before the Salon opened. Today in France, art previews are still called the *vernissage*.

The Salon of 1879—The Preview. Notice the artist on the left applying a final coat of varnish to his painting.

Where could the Impressionists show their work? Friends and supporters donated space. For the first exhibition in 1874, a photographer named T. F. Nadar offered his studio. The show was a complete flop. None of the thirty-one artists sold a painting. One review sniffed, "When children amuse themselves with paper and colors they do better." Despite the criticism, the Impressionists held eight exhibitions between 1874 and 1886.

Were the Impressionists good friends? One of the Impressionists, Pierre-Auguste Renoir, said, "We were all one group when we first started out. We stood shoulder to shoulder and we encouraged each other."

As young artists, the Impressionists gathered at Parisian cafés and spent holidays painting together at country inns. They painted each other's families, girlfriends, and friends. But they also argued and gossiped. There were rivalries because they were all vying for the same dealers. Yet, in times of personal trouble, they took care of one another. They loaned money, shared food and board, and bought each other's paintings. In the 1880s, however, the group began to drift apart. Some started families and moved out of Paris. Others tried new ways of painting. Only a few stayed in close touch.

Up to your elbows in French art terms? The mnemonic **ELBOW** might help you to think about the qualities of Impressionism. When you look around your museum gallery, think:

E veryday life
L ight
B rushstrokes
O utdoor painting
W eather and atmosphere

The "Inside" Impressionists

   Some of the Impressionists preferred to paint indoor scenes. Manet, Morisot, Degas, and Cassatt all captured a certain feeling about turn-of-the-century life in the interior spaces of France. Manet pioneered a new approach to painting by focusing on contemporary life. Once he had made the break, the others experienced the freedom to choose their own subject matter and develop their own style. While Morisot painted portraits of friends and family, Degas found inspiration in the dance halls and theaters of Paris. Cassatt specialized in painting intimate portraits of mothers and children.

Off the Wall with

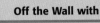

Edouard Manet
(January 25, 1832–1883)

Edouard Manet photographed by Nadar.

The son of a Parisian judge, Edouard Manet is sometimes called the "Father of Impressionism." Yet he never exhibited with the Impressionists, preferring to show in the official Salon. Manet paved the way for the Impressionists because he was a painter of modern life. Although he had academic art training and routinely copied the old masters in the Louvre Museum, Manet believed artists should paint their own times—*their* cafés, bars, and dance halls. He shocked viewers by turning classical subjects into everyday scenes. Manet's use of rough patches of color, sometimes applied with a palette knife instead of shading, encouraged the Impressionists to paint freely. Manet's paintings are known for their rich blacks and browns.

Palette knife A palette knife is a small, narrow spatula. It is used to mix and spread paint.

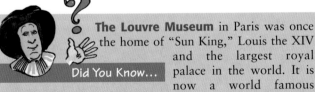

Did You Know... **The Louvre Museum** in Paris was once the home of "Sun King," Louis the XIV and the largest royal palace in the world. It is now a world famous museum, taking up forty acres of space and containing eight miles of galleries!

Courtyard, Louvre Museum. Today visitors enter the museum through a glass pyramid leading underground.

Edouard Manet

Edouard Manet, *Le Déjeuner sur l'Herbe (Luncheon on the Grass),* 1863.

Manet's Shocking Luncheon

In 1863, two thousand artists, including Manet, were turned down from the Salon! There was such protest from the rejected artists that Emperor Napoleon III (1808–1873) set up an exhibit just for them. It was called *Le Salon des Refusés* (Salon of the Rejected). Manet's entry was a seven by nine foot painting called *Luncheon on the Grass*. It shocked the art world.

Did You Know... The woman in Manet's painting was his favorite model, Victorine Meurent. Eighteen years old at the time, she was his model for thirteen years. She, too, was an artist. Look for her red hair and signature black neck cord in other paintings by Manet.

A Closer Look

- Look for Manet's blacks and browns. He is known for his rich, velvety black.
- Check for broad strokes of paint where Manet may have used a palette knife.

Edouard Manet

Engraving after Raphael's *The Judgment of Paris*. Look at the lower right-hand corner. Manet copied the poses of Greek gods from this Italian Renaissance engraving, but dressed them in French street clothes.

Why was it shocking? Manet had turned a scene from a well-known Renaissance painting of Greek gods into a modern Parisian picnic! What's more, he painted a naked woman in the middle of the picnic. Not a goddess, but a present-day woman! She didn't look perfect like a classical sculpture. She looked real. The men (posed by Manet's brother and a friend) were wearing Parisian street clothes. The style was shocking, too. Manet painted *Le Déjeuner sur l'Herbe* with free, thick brush-strokes. Skin tones show no modeling. Instead, the color was not smoothly blended, as it would have been in an academic painting, but patchy. The men's faces and the naked woman herself look relatively flat.

Word Wizard

Sandwich It's possible that the people who posed for Manet might have eaten sandwiches at their picnic. People had been eating sandwiches for around 100 years! An eighteenth-century Englishman, John Montague, Earl of Sandwich, once played cards for twenty-four hours straight until somebody gave him sliced meat between two pieces of toast. He took a break to eat it and the sandwich was named.

Edouard Manet

ART SCOOP

Manet's hidden treasure During wars, some countries have hidden their national treasures for safekeeping. After World War II, the U.S. army found some of Manet's paintings buried deep inside a German salt mine!

Manet's *Wintergarden* hanging in a German salt mine.

Art Oops!

Manet's cutting edge Manet made a painting of a bullfight for the Salon of 1864. The critics didn't like it so Manet cut it into pieces. Today, one piece hangs in a New York museum and another, *Dead Toreador,* is in Washington's National Gallery.

Another sneaky move! Before World War II, France moved its art treasures to the safety of castles outside Paris. On the night of August 28, 1939, the world's most famous painting, Leonardo da Vinci's *Mona Lisa,* left her home at the Louvre Museum. The painting was strapped to an ambulance stretcher in a custom-made case and rode at the head of an eight-truck convoy

Paintmate Manet was copying a painting in the Louvre when he first met **Edgar Degas.** They remained friends for twenty-one years. Lifelong Parisians, they were rivals in art but admired each other's work. Their families were also friends. Degas painted eight portraits of Manet, one of which caused a fight. After Manet died, his daughter gave one of his paintings to Degas.

Off the Wall with

Berthe Morisot
(January 14, 1841–1895)

Berthe Morisot, 1869.

Born into a family that descended from eighteenth-century court painter Jean-Honoré Fragonard, Berthe Morisot always wanted to be an artist. She started drawing lessons at a time when it was considered a "catastrophe" for a woman to study art. Morisot had paintings accepted at the Salon, but gave it up to join and exhibit with the Impressionist group. She painted many indoor scenes of family and friends. She is known for a silvery quality of light, a feathery brushstroke, and a delicate touch. Morisot was in every Impressionist exhibition but one. She was an active member of the group, holding many gatherings at her house in Paris. Morisot married Edouard Manet's younger brother Eugene.

ART SCOOP

Mother goes best Morisot had to take an escort whenever she wanted to copy the Old Masters at the Louvre. Her mother came with her and knitted while she worked.

Why can't I be more like a man? The diary of an artist who painted in Paris at the same time as Morisot describes the sheltered life of a woman in nineteenth-century Paris. She writes,

"What I long for is the freedom of going about alone…of stopping and looking at the artistic shops, of entering churches and museums…chaperoned as I am…in order to go to the Louvre, I must wait for my carriage, my lady companion and family."

Berthe Morisot

- How long did it take you to see the white dog in the foreground of *Dining Room*?
- Notice Morisot's long, feathery brushstrokes, especially on the girl's apron. Now think of Manet's broad strokes. What a difference!
- Look for indoor scenes in your gallery.

Off limits Berthe Morisot and her fellow Impressionist, Mary Cassatt, could not paint the same subjects as their male counterparts. It was improper for well-brought-up women to be seen at cafés, backstage at the theater, in train stations, or on city streets. It was easier for them to paint scenes closer to home, such as family and friends in their houses and gardens.

Paintmate Morisot met **Edouard Manet** at the Louvre Museum in 1867 when she was copying a painting. They became lifelong friends, and Manet painted her portrait fourteen times. Manet, however, sometimes annoyed Morisot. One time Morisot asked Manet to look at one of her paintings that was going to the Salon jury. Grabbing Morisot's palette and brush, Manet started changing her work: first a dab to a skirt, then to the head and hands. "Cracking a thousand jokes, he laughed like a madman," she wrote her sister. "I found it agonizing."

Off the Wall with

Edgar Degas
(July 19, 1834–1917)

The son of a Parisian banker, Edgar Degas exhibited in seven of the eight Impressionist shows. He focused primarily on the human figure, although he also painted some outdoor scenes. Degas attended L'Ecole des Beaux-Arts and never abandoned the classical training he received there. His compositions are carefully worked out and his figures precisely drawn. Planning his paintings, he said, took "the cunning of a crime."

Portrait of Edgar Degas by Barnes.

Degas, like the other Impressionists, was committed to painting modern life. He was the only Impressionist to paint the effects of light—limelights and gaslights—at night. He is best known for his paintings and pastels of the dance corps of the Paris Opera. But he also did portraits, scenes of racetracks, and women bathing or combing their hair. His compositions are unusual and show the influence of photography and Japanese art.

Pastel Once called "the powder of a butterfly wing," pastel is powdered pigment shaped into a stick and bound with gum. It is used for drawing but can be blended and smudged. It is sometimes called pastel paint. Degas was a master of pastel.

Word Wizard

Limelight You may have heard the expression to "hog the limelight," which means to enjoy being the center of attention. Limelights were burning cylinders made of lime that were used to light the Paris theater and opera before there was electricity.

Edgar Degas

Edgar Degas, *Waiting: Dancer and Woman with Umbrella on a Bench,* circa 1882. This young dancer is rubbing a sore foot. The woman sitting next to her is probably her mother.

A Closer Look

• Notice the diagonal line in the floor and bench of *Waiting*. Find another diagonal.

• Look at the Japanese woodblock print on page 40. Compare it with Degas' *Waiting*. How are they similar? Both have a bird's-eye viewpoint, two women, cropped subject matter, and strong diagonal lines.

• Can you find any mothers in Degas's work? Women combing their hair, bathing, dancing?

• What time of day is it in a Degas painting? How can you tell?

• Check the greens in Degas's paintings. It has been said that some of Degas's colors give the feeling of a tart apple in your mouth. Can you find a Degas painting that gives you that feeling?

• Look for a Degas painting with an image cut off at the margin.

• Look for pastel drawings by Degas.

Edgar Degas

Degas and Sculpture

Degas sculpted all his life, but few people knew it. In 1881 he made a small painted wax figurine of Marie van Goetham, a fourteen-year-old ballerina. It was shown at the sixth Impressionist exhibition. The sculpture was fitted with a real horsehair wig, satin ribbon, satin ballet shoes, and cotton tutu. After Degas' death, many more wax sculptures were found in his studio. No one had known about them. Degas had done them for his own pleasure.

Edgar Degas, *The Little Dancer*. This sculpture of Marie van Goetham was the only sculpture Degas ever exhibited. Some people did not like the dancer's clothes or her face. One critic wrote that she looked "vicious."

Did You Know...

A dancer's life The Paris Opera had its own dance company. Most ballet dancers started as apprentices around age seven or eight at the State Opera School. Many of the dancers came from humble families; they walked to school, ate a cold lunch, and worked all day. For several years, they studied for long hours without pay. When they were around ten years old, if they had passed all their exams, they began to earn a small salary. Mothers managed their daughters' careers. A successful ballerina could make more money than her father! Many of Degas's dance pictures show mothers waiting or arranging their daughter's costume.

Edgar Degas

The effect of the camera The Impressionists studied photographs for new ideas. Some of them referred to photographs for their paintings. They liked the spontaneity of cropped images and motion-blurring. Monet owned four cameras and Degas owned one.

George Eastman, *Mr. Nadar, Place de l'Opéra, Paris,* 1890. Photographer T. F. Nadar poses in front of the new Paris Opera house in one of the first snapshots ever taken.

Notice how the ladies' long skirts in the photo are cropped (cut off). Some Impressionists, like Degas, liked to crop subjects in their paintings, too.

A Closer Look

Make a circle with your first finger and thumb. Pretend it is the viewfinder of a camera. Focus on a friend or painting. Move the viewfinder a little to the right. You have just cropped your subject!

Did You Know...

The first hand-held snapshot camera was available in 1888. George Eastman had developed it and called it the #1 Kodak. The camera used a roll of film that took 100 round pictures. Eastman chose the name *Kodak* because it was short and could be pronounced in every language.

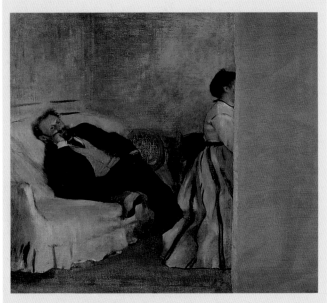

Edgar Degas, *M. and Mme. Edouard Manet,* circa 1868–1869. This is the famous painting that caused a fight. Notice the blank canvas where Manet cut out his wife.

Degas and the Slashed Canvas

Manet and Degas made several paintings of each other. In 1867, Degas did a double portrait of Manet and his wife, Suzanne, playing the piano. When the portrait was finished, Manet did not like the way his wife looked and cut her half of the painting off. Degas found out and was furious. He reclaimed the painting and added a piece of empty canvas to replace what Manet had cut. Eventually, the two artists patched up their fight, and Degas kept the portrait in his drawing room until he died.

Degas in America

Degas lived in New Orleans from 1872 to 1873 while visiting his cousins. While he was there, cotton was still king in the South, and he painted *The New Orleans Cotton Exchange*. This was the first of Degas's paintings to be bought for a public art collection. Today, the house where Degas lived is a museum.

Impressionists who sculpted Edgar Degas and Pierre-Auguste Renoir made sculptures as well as paintings. Degas made wax sculptures for his own enjoyment. Many were cast into bronze after he died. Renoir took up sculpture in the last years of his life. Their sculptures can be seen in museums today.

Poems to a Parrot?

Degas also wrote poetry. You can read a poem he wrote to his friend Mary Cassatt's beloved green parrot, Coco. It is called *"Parrot."*

ART SCOOP

Studio secrets Degas did not allow his studio to be dusted—*ever*—except for the path from the door to the model's stand. He was afraid that his canvases and frames would be damaged.

Paintmate Degas and **Mary Cassatt** were friends for forty years. He painted eight portraits of her, and she painted one of him. He helped her with her drawing technique and printmaking. She urged her American friends to buy his work.

Mary Cassatt
(May 22, 1845–1926)

Joseph Durand-Ruel, *Madame Joseph Durand-Ruel, Mary Cassatt , an unidentified friend, and Marie-Louise Durand-Ruel,* 1910.

The daughter of a Philadelphia banker, Mary Cassatt was the only American to exhibit with the Impressionists. At the age of twenty, she left the Pennsylvania Academy of Fine Arts and moved to Paris, where she studied art with Jean-Léon Gérôme, a popular artist of his day. Impressionist Edgar Degas noticed her work at the Paris Salon and invited her to join the fourth Impressionist exhibit. From then on, Cassatt was part of the Impressionist group, showing with them and urging Americans to buy their work.

Cassatt mainly painted interior scenes. Using family and friends as models, her favorite theme was motherhood. She painted many pastels and oils on this subject with a quiet tenderness.

In 1890, an exhibition of Japanese woodblock prints in Paris inspired Cassatt to try printmaking. She finished more than 200 prints, proving to be a gifted printmaker. Many of these prints show the influence of Japanese woodblocks.

Cataracts in both eyes finally slowed down Cassatt's work, and by the last decade of her life, she had stopped painting. Cassatt remained a U.S. citizen, although she lived in France for more than fifty years and was buried there.

FAMILY FIRST After Cassatt moved to France, her parents and sister left America to live permanently with her in Paris. Cassatt spent almost twenty years looking after them during their illnesses.

Mary Cassatt

Mary Cassatt, *Mother and Child,* circa 1890.

A Closer Look

• Is there a Cassatt portrait of a mother and child in your gallery?

• Look for mothers' hands in Cassatt's portraits. Describe them. They are probably strong and caring hands. Look at children's hands, too.

• Look at your own hands. Put them in the same position as those in the painting. Does it change how you feel? Try this with other paintings.

JAPANESE PRINTS AND IMPRESSIONISM

After Japan was opened to the West in 1854, Paris shops began to sell Japanese woodblock prints. The Impressionists liked their unusual compositions. Cassatt and other Impressionists began to use Japanese design techniques in their own work. Some features that the Impressionists borrowed included simplified lines, diagonals, images cut

Totoya Hokkei, *The Jewel that Shines at Night,* early 1830s.

off at the margins, surprising viewpoints, decorative patterning, and bird's-eye views. Cassatt, Degas, Monet, and van Gogh were all influenced by Japanese woodblock prints.

A Closer Look

• Look for diagonal lines, cropped edges, bird's-eye views, and other unusual viewpoints in an Impressionist Gallery.
• Ask someone at the Information Desk if the museum has a collection of Japanese prints.

Secrets in the woodshed During World War I, German officers used Cassatt's country house as a command post. Cassatt hid her works under a pile of logs in the woodshed.

Paintmate Cassatt first became familiar with **Edgar Degas** by staring at his paintings. Although she hadn't yet met him, she used to flatten her nose against an art gallery window to admire his work. "It changed my life," she said later. Little did she know that he would become one of her closest friends. Cassatt and Degas had a forty-one year friendship. She called him "her oldest friend in Paris." Before she died, Cassatt destroyed all of Degas's letters to her. Probably no one will ever know the exact nature of their relationship.

Plein-air Impressionists

    The group of artists in this section did most of their painting outdoors, and were known as plein-air painters. Although they were not the first French artists to go outdoors, the Impressionists were the first French artists to start and finish paintings outdoors most of the time. Monet, Renoir, and Sisley started painting outside together in 1864.

Pierre-Auguste Renoir, *Monet Painting in His Garden at Argenteuil,* 1873. Notice the portable easel and parasol.

The following inventions made it possible for the plein-air painters to work outside:

- Collapsible tin tubes of paint were invented in England in 1841. They enabled the Impressionists to paint outside for the entire day. Before tubes, artists had to squeeze paints stored in sacks made from pig's bladders. This was a messy process and the paints dried up fast. Renoir said, "Without tubes of paint, there would have been no Impressionism."

- The firl, or square metal brace, clamped paintbrush hairs stiff and square. This brush let artists apply thick paint.

- Chemical pigments gave the Impressionists brighter colors to use.

- Portable easels were lightweight and easy to carry outside.

Word Wizard

Easel The word *easel* comes from the Dutch word *ezel,* meaning "donkey." An art easel's beastly burden is to carry paintings.

Off the Wall with

Camille Pissarro
(July 10, 1830–1903)

Camille Pissarro was the oldest Impressionist and the only one to show in every Impressionist exhibition. When he was twenty-five, Pissarro came to Paris from the West Indies where he met fellow Impressionists Monet, Renoir, and Sisley. Committed to painting outdoors, Pissarro's paintings are rooted in the countryside. He was less interested in passing cloud effects and water reflections than other Impressionists. Rather, his paintings reflect the solid forms and seasonal rhythms of country life. His subjects are peasants and animals, orchards, planted fields, and country roads. He used broken brushstrokes and small, thick daubs of pure color to build form and give structure to his paintings.

The Impressionists looked to Pissarro as a kindly father figure and teacher. Fellow painter Mary Cassatt said that Pissarro "could have taught stones to draw correctly." His eagerness to help the other artists unified the group.

Camille Pissarro with Julie, Paul Emile, and Jeanne in the Orchard at Eragny, 1897. Camille Pissarro with his wife and two of his seven children. Notice his portable easel on wheels.

Camille Pissarro

Camille Pissarro, *Haying Time,* 1892. Pissarro often painted the landscape around his home at Eragny, two hours north of Paris.

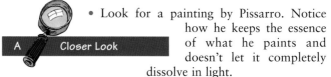

A Closer Look

• Look for a painting by Pissarro. Notice how he keeps the essence of what he paints and doesn't let it completely dissolve in light.

• Look for a tree that disappears into the light and air of a landscape. Do you prefer solid forms or airy forms?

• What colors does Pissarro put next to each other in his paintings? How many colors make up a face or hat?

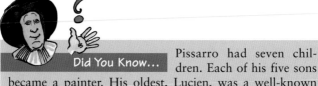

Did You Know... Pissarro had seven children. Each of his five sons became a painter. His oldest, Lucien, was a well-known English Impressionist.

ART SCOOP

Paintings underfoot While Pissarro was in London during the Franco-Prussian war, Prussians occupied his home outside Paris. His kitchen was used as a sheep pen. Of the 1,500 paintings Pissarro left behind in his studio, only forty survived. Many had been used to carpet the muddy garden.

What was the Franco-Prussian war? A brief power struggle between France and Prussia, Germany's biggest state. French Emperor Napoleon III declared war on Prussia in July 1870, but was captured six weeks later. The Prussians surrounded Paris, cutting off the food supply and causing a four-month famine. The French surrendered in January 1871, and had to pay the equivalent of one billion dollars to the Germans. Of the Impressionists, Manet, Degas, and Renoir served in the war.

Paintmate Pissarro and **Cézanne** were friends for ten years. Pissarro taught Cézanne to paint outdoors in the Impressionist style. While he was learning, Cézanne set up his easel next to Pissarro's and painted the same scene. The two artists painted each other many times. Pissarro owned more than forty of Cézanne's works.

Man of the moment: an Impressionist art dealer
Pissarro and Claude Monet met Paris art dealer Paul Durand-Ruel as young artists. Durand-Ruel soon became the group's main financial support and advocate. When the public scorned the works of the Impressionists, Durand-Ruel bought their paintings and organized exhibitions. Renoir said, "Without him we would not have survived."

Claude Monet
(February 14, 1840–1926)

Claude Monet by Sardnal, 1897.

Claude Monet made more than 2,000 paintings in a career lasting almost seventy years. He grew up in Le Havre, where artist Jean Boudin introduced him to outdoor painting. Monet said that the change brought about by painting outside was as "though a veil had been torn from his eyes." From then on, the countryside became his studio.

At age nineteen, Monet moved to Paris where he met Renoir and Sisley. More than any artist in the group, Monet made a lifelong commitment to Impressionism—to capturing the fleeting effects of light outdoors. Monet preferred painting landscapes to people. Of all the Impressionists, he was the most determined plein-air painter. Gales and rain—even snow drifts—didn't stop him. Sometimes he dug trenches in the ground to prop up his canvases. For water-based views, he used a studio boat.

In the 1880s, Monet started creating series of paintings. He wanted to show how light affects the same object at different times of day. He finished fifteen haystacks, eleven poplar trees, and twenty cathedrals. In 1883, he moved to Giverny, fifty-five miles south of Paris, where he built a Japanese-inspired water garden. A series he painted of its waterlilies occupied him until he died.

Claude Monet

Claude Monet, *Haystacks,* 1889. This painting was done in a field near Monet's house in Giverny.

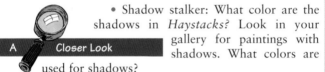

* Shadow stalker: What color are the shadows in *Haystacks?* Look in your gallery for paintings with shadows. What colors are used for shadows?

* How many kinds of brushstrokes can you find in one Monet painting? Do any of the following words describe them? thick, square, sketchy, comma-like, circular, stumpy, fine, grooved.

* Find one primary color next to its best friend complement in a Monet painting.

* Does Monet paint any lines in his paintings?

Hey! Haystacks Also known as grainstacks, Monet's haystacks were not piles of hay loosely pitched to feed passing cattle. They were carefully bound stalks built to last months. Their conical tops were fifteen to twenty feet tall. Monet's haystack series happened by chance. While painting one haystack, the light changed, and he sent his stepdaughter back to the house for another canvas...and another. A series was begun.

All Natural Ingredients X-rays show traces of sand and shell embedded in Monet's paintings done outside at the beach!

ART **S** COOP

Paying to paint While Monet was painting his series of poplar trees, he heard that the trees were about to be sold for lumber at auction. He asked a timber dealer to bid whatever price it would take to buy them. He would pay him back. The trees were bought for Monet, and he finished his series of fifteen poplars.

Beans and nude models? When they roomed together, Monet and Renoir were able to scrape up just enough money to pay for a nude studio model. To save money, they cooked their meals while she posed so as not to waste heat.

Paintmate Monet and **Renoir** were friends for fifty-seven years. They were closest during the 1870s, when they shared a studio and housing outside of Paris. During this time, they were penniless. Monet wrote in a letter, "Renoir brings us bread from his mother's house so we don't die of hunger.…For a week, no bread, no wine, no fire for cooking, no light. It's terrible." Renoir told friends that he was hardly painting because he couldn't afford paints. The two artists got by on beans unless one of their customers, a grocer, paid them in food. Still, Renoir remembered that he had "never been happier." Visitors to Monet's home said that he kept three paintings by Renoir in his bedroom.

Claude Monet

Halt the Trains!
It's Monsieur Monet!

Monet liked trains. Early one morning in 1877, he told his friend Renoir that he wanted to paint the trains at the Gare Saint-Lazare when they were starting up. He wanted it foggy, "a regular dream world." So Monet dressed in his finest clothes, including a shirt with lace-lined cuffs, grabbed his gold-headed cane, and set off for the railroad station. He handed the station master his card which said, *Claude Monet, painter.* Although the station master knew nothing about artists, he was struck by this well-dressed gentleman. He ordered the trains delayed and the platforms cleared. Then he ordered the engines to start. Monet had all the steam he wanted and the station to himself. He made eight paintings on this theme.

Claude Monet, *The Gare Saint-Lazare: Arrival of a Train*, 1877. Monet painted the smoke from the trains in the impasto manner, with short, thick brushstrokes.

Alfred Sisley
(October 30, 1839–1899)

Alfred Sisley.

The son of an English mother and half-French father, Alfred Sisley spent most of his life in France. He met Monet and Renoir at Gleyre's atelier in Paris, and with them formed the original group of Impressionists who started painting together outside. A modest man, Sisley was the least known of the Impressionist group. Nearly always penniless, his paintings found few buyers while he was alive.

Sisley was content to live and paint most of his life near the forest of Fontainebleau. His favorite subjects were scenes of villages near his home, their streets, paths, orchards, and rivers. Sisley showed little interest in the human figure. The sky was his passion, and he used a low horizon line to allow for it. He also liked painting snow, mist, and water reflections. Sisley's paintings have a sense of calm and a delicate touch.

Monsters of Fontainebleau The forest of Fontainebleau, thirty-five miles south of Paris, was known for deep gorges and strange rock formations. Some people believed that monsters lived there. Fontainebleau was a popular day trip from Paris by train. Visitors picnicked, saw the summer palace of French kings, and watched artists paint outdoors!

Did You Know...

Alfred Sisley

Alfred Sisley, *Bougival*, 1876.

A Closer Look

• Look at Sisley's sky in *Bougival*. Is the horizon line high or low?

• Look in your gallery for four canvases to see where the land and sky meet. The most common meeting place is usually in the middle of the painting.

• How would you paint a sunny, clear, warm day?

• Look for a painting in your museum by Alfred Sisley. Are there people in it? Is there a sense of calm?

ART SCOOP

A sweet deal One of Sisley's best patrons was a pastry chef! Hyacinthe Eugene Murer owned twenty-eight of Sisley's paintings. Sisley, Pissarro, Renoir, and Monet ate at his tearoom regularly.

Paintmate Sisley spent more time painting with **Monet** than any other artist. Before his death, Sisley asked Monet to look after his two children. After Sisley died, Monet arranged an auction of unsold paintings in Sisley's studio to raise money for them.

Off the Wall with

Pierre-Auguste Renoir
(February 25, 1841–1919)

Renoir was born in Limoges to a tailor and a seamstress. He started work at age thirteen in a Paris porcelain factory. There he became skilled at painting floral bouquets and classical nudes on vases and dessert services. Five years later, he lost his job to machine-produced painting. But he never lost the light touch or palette of pinks, yellows, blues, and greens he had used to paint porcelain.

In 1862, Renoir met Monet and Sisley at Gleyre's atelier in Paris and started to paint plein air. Renoir said paintings should be "likable, joyous and pretty." It is this *joie*

Renoir in His Studio, circa 1912.

de vivre (joy of life) that sets his paintings apart from other Impressionists. His favorite subjects were young women, children, and scenes of Parisian life. Renoir painted with thin paint and feathery, comma-shaped brushstrokes. Claiming later on that he was really "a figure painter," he turned away from Impressionism to paint more solid forms. In old age, Renoir suffered from arthritis, but he continued to work with paintbrushes strapped to his hands.

Painting the Town Red

Guidebooks from Renoir's time called Paris "the capital of pleasure." It offered concerts, opera, cafés, outdoor dancing, carriage or train rides, picnics in the park or by the river, rowing, canoeing, horse racing, and shopping at the new department stores. But, if you were invited to a court ball over a long weekend, beware! You needed to pack "twenty dresses, five gowns for tea, and a hunting outfit."

Pierre-Auguste Renoir

Pierre-Auguste Renoir, *Luncheon of the Boating Party,* 1881. Many of Renoir's friends posed for this painting. The woman with the red flowered hat is Renoir's future wife, Aline Charigot.

A Closer Look

- Locate a puppy in the foreground and a boat in the background of *Boating Party*. What is happening between the two areas?
- Find glass, fabric, fruit, and hats in your gallery. What colors has the artist used to paint them?
- Look for the little commas that are typical of Renoir's feathery brushwork.
- Think of **ELBOW** (page 24) while looking at the *Boating Party*. What is the weather like?

ART SCOOP

Stakeout Café Renoir liked to sketch passers-by from a certain café. Using his brother Edmond as a decoy, he found a sneaky way to make them pause long enough for him to draw. Edmond would approach to ask directions to a faraway place. While they explained, Renoir would draw them from the café.

Renoir's Nose for Boots!

As a young artist, Renoir needed boots. He agreed to paint a portrait of a bootmaker's wife in return for a pair. Every time he thought the portrait was finished, a member of her family would complain that something was wrong. Finally someone said, "Don't you think she has a much shorter nose than that?" Renoir wanted his boots so he gave her the nose of Madame de Pompadour, the beautiful eighteenth-century mistress of King Louis XV. Then everyone was happy!

Paintmate Born the same year as Renoir, **Berthe Morisot** became one of his closest friends. Renoir visited the Morisots regularly and he painted their daughter, Julie. After her husband died, Morisot asked Renoir to be Julie's guardian.

Did You Know... *Paris, City of Light* French Emperor Napoleon III wanted to make Paris the showcase of Europe. In 1852, he asked architect Baron Haussmann to give the city a bright, new look. Three hundred miles of dark, medieval streets and buildings soon gave way to eighty-five miles of wide, tree-lined boulevards. Fancy apartment buildings and "starburst" intersections replaced much of the old city. A new opera house, the biggest in the world, with a stage for 450 performers, was the pride of Paris. Many Impressionist paintings show the new Paris.

Pierre-Auguste Renoir, *Les Grands Boulevards,* 1875.

The Post-Impressionists

Who were the Post-Impressionists? They were artists who, disenchanted with the pretty picture surfaces and fleeting effects of Impressionism, wanted to put structure back into their art. Using simplified forms, Cézanne and Seurat labored to create solid compositions and deep space, while van Gogh and Gauguin used flat shapes, broad outlines, and vivid color to express their feelings. The term Post-Impressionism was first used in 1910 at a London art show for Cézanne, Gauguin, van Gogh, and Seurat who were billed as the Post-Impressionists. The term now applies to artists painting around 1890–1914, whose work shows a reaction to Impressionism.

Off the Wall with

Paul Cézanne
(January 19, 1839–1906)

Paul Cézanne was born in Aix in the south of France. His father wanted him to be a lawyer or in the family banking business. Cézanne tried both, but his heart was in neither. Instead he sketched and wrote poetry on the bank's ledger:

My banking father shudders to see
Born in his counting house depths a painter-to-be.

Eventually, his father agreed to let him study art at the Académie Suisse in Paris. One of his fellow students was Camille Pissarro, who introduced him to Impressionism.

Paul Cézanne, *Self-Portrait with a Beret,* circa 1898–1899.

Cézanne began to paint outdoors with Pissarro and to use brighter colors, but he felt that Impressionism lacked structure. His goal, he said, was "to make something solid and durable out of Impressionism."

Using squarish patches of color to convey shadow and light, he worked on conveying the structure and permanence of objects. "Nothing matters but volume," he said. Cézanne entered two Impressionist exhibitions, but eventually returned to Aix where he worked out of a studio attached to his family home.

Paul Cézanne

Paul Cézanne, *Basket of Apples*, circa 1895.

- Find an apple in Cézanne's still life. Does it look good enough to eat? Cézanne was interested in how to make objects look heavy. Look at the tablecloth. Notice how he has given it structure. The folds look like mountains.
- Look for a still life in your gallery. Imagine how the artist moved his or her hand to paint each detail.
- What are popular subjects for still life in your gallery?

Apples or Eve? Shy with women models, Cézanne said that fruit was easier to paint. Fruit stayed still and didn't mind posing for hours. Cézanne was known to ask models to sit 100 times for a painting. Sometimes he scolded, "Be still like an apple!" It is not surprising that Cézanne had a hard time getting models. He often ended up using his wife.

Paul Cézanne

The Artist's Hand

This is an example of Cézanne's handwriting.

It has been reproduced on a computer. He did this sketch of an apple too.

This is his signature: *Cézanne*. Can you match it with a signature in one of his paintings?

ART SCOOP

A famous basket of apples   When Cézanne was thirteen years old, he defended a skinny boy with glasses who was being teased at school. The little boy gave Cézanne a basket of apples for helping him. The boy grew up to be a famous French writer named Emile Zola. Some people think that Cézanne painted apples as a symbol of their friendship

Art Oops!

Cézanne sometimes despaired over his work. On one visit, his dealer, Ambroise Vollard, found that he had tossed paintings out his window into a tree.

Paintmate   Cézanne met **Pissarro** in Paris and described himself as a "pupil of Pissarro." He said of him, "...he was a father to me. He was a man to be consulted, something like *le bon dieu* (the good lord)." When Cézanne's son was born, Pissarro invited Cézanne to move out of Paris to be near his family.

Off the Wall with

Paul Gauguin
(June 7, 1848–1903)

The son of a French journalist, Paul Gauguin spent his early childhood in Lima, Peru. After schooling and navy service in France, he joined a bank in Paris. But he also took art courses at night and met the Impressionists. Before long, he was painting outside with Pissarro and Cézanne. At age twenty-five, Gauguin quit finance to paint full-time.

After a painting visit to Brittany, Gauguin lost interest in

Paul Gauguin in Oceania.

painting landscapes outdoors. He began to use dark outlines, decorative patterns, and flat, unnatural colors to convey spiritual themes. In 1891, tired of what he called the "hubbub of life in Europe," he left France to seek "calmness and art" in Tahiti. Aided by a state grant for an "artistic mission," Gauguin lived in a wooden hut eating fish, roots, and fruit. Except for two years back in France, Gauguin spent the rest of his life in Tahiti and the Marquesas Islands. In addition to painting, he made woodblock prints, sculpture, and pottery.

What do Gauguin's paintings mean? Gauguin thought paintings should reflect the artist's inner life and emotions. Some of his unnatural colors suggest that his paintings are dreams or visions. He said he was looking for the "mysterious centers of thought."

Petticoats and tablecloths Gauguin's son, Emil, remembers how upset his mother got with Gauguin for using her best tablecloth as a canvas and petticoats as paint rags!

Paul Gauguin

Paul Gauguin, *Woman of the Mango,* 1892. This painting was owned by Degas. He bought it at a sale to help Gauguin raise money to return to Tahiti. The woman is Gauguin's young Tahitian bride, Teha'amana.

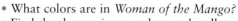

A Closer Look

• What colors are in *Woman of the Mango*?
• Find the three primary colors: red, yellow, and blue.
• Do you see patterning? simplified form? bright color? dark outlines?
• Find a painting of a place that looks like "paradise" to you.

Did You Know...

Tahiti is an island in the South Pacific Ocean that belongs to France. It is part of a group of islands that make up Oceania. One hundred years before Gauguin arrived, William Bligh, Captain of *H.M.S. Bounty*, visited Tahiti. *Mutiny on the Bounty* is a true story of Bligh's adventures after he was cast overboard by his crew into the South Pacific Ocean.

Paintmate Gauguin met **Vincent van Gogh** in Paris. Van Gogh had dreamed of starting a "Studio of the South" for Impressionists. He invited Gauguin to live and share studio space with him in his yellow house in southern France. To honor Gauguin's visit, van Gogh made a painting of yellow sunflowers for Gauguin's guest bedroom. While they lived together, Gauguin did the cooking and van Gogh shopped. Both artists finished many paintings while they were in Arles.

Off the Wall with

Vincent van Gogh
(March 30, 1853–1890)

Vincent van Gogh, *Self-Portrait Dedicated to Paul Gauguin,* 1888. Van Gogh inscribed this portrait to "my friend Paul Gauguin."

A painter for only ten years, Vincent van Gogh was born in the Netherlands, the son of a minister. After working with an art dealer and later as a missionary for coal miners in Belgium, at the age of twenty-seven, van Gogh decided to study art. He studied in Antwerp and then in Paris where he met Pissarro, Monet, Gauguin, and Degas. Contact with the Impressionists changed his painting. He lightened his colors and used smaller brushstrokes.

Claiming, however, to need the "light" of the South, van Gogh moved to Arles in southern France. It was here that he did his best-known work. Van Gogh's paintings are marked by thick paint, strong outlines, and bold colors, which he uses for expressive purposes. His twisted brushstrokes make objects come alive. Van Gogh painted forty-three self portraits in the last four years of his life.

Vincent van Gogh

Vincent van Gogh, *Bedroom at Arles,* 1888.

A Closer Look

• Can you find van Gogh's shaving bowl and water jug under the white mirror?

• Look for yellow in van Gogh's paintings.

• Look in your gallery for other artists' yellows. Compare their yellow with van Gogh's.

• Using your finger in the air, copy his brushstrokes. Are they like flames, commas, spirals, dots, twists?

• Van Gogh did not sign all of his paintings. When he did, he only signed his first name. See if your museum has a van Gogh signature.

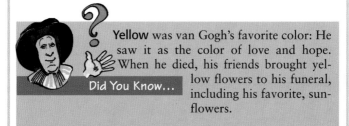

Did You Know...

Yellow was van Gogh's favorite color: He saw it as the color of love and hope. When he died, his friends brought yellow flowers to his funeral, including his favorite, sunflowers.

ART SCOOP

Van Gogh's friendship with Gauguin ended during Gauguin's stay with van Gogh in Arles. After two months, van Gogh and Gauguin had an argument, and Gauguin left for a hotel. That night, van Gogh cut off his own ear. Two days later, Gauguin moved back to Paris.

Why did van Gogh and Gauguin fight? Van Gogh may have guessed that Gauguin planned to move out early. If so, van Gogh would have been disappointed. He hoped Gauguin would stay at least six months.

Why did van Gogh cut off his own ear? No one knows. Some people think he was punishing himself for fighting with Gauguin. Others say he was trying to silence "voices" he heard.

A painting that flew the coop People did not appreciate van Gogh's paintings during his life. A portrait he gave his doctor in Arles was used by the doctor's family to plug a hole in their chicken coop. Today it is one of the treasures of the Pushkin Museum in Moscow. *Irises,* another van Gogh painting unsold in his lifetime, was sold at auction for 49 million dollars in 1989.

Paintmate Van Gogh was devoted to his younger brother, **Theo,** who was an art dealer in Paris. He wrote him more than 650 letters. These were published in a book, *Letters to Theo.* Theo helped Vincent by sending him a monthly allowance and asking art dealers to promote his work. Theo died six months after Vincent. The two brothers are buried next to each other in Auvers, France.

Off the Wall with

Georges Pierre Seurat
(December 2, 1859–1891)

The son of a Parisian civil servant, Georges Seurat produced only six major paintings in his life. After studying at L'Ecole des Beaux-Arts, he worked on black-and-white tonal drawings. But Seurat's goal was to do "something new, an art entirely my own." In 1886 he stunned the art world with his painting, *A Sunday on the Grande Jatte.* This huge painting was the star attraction at the final Impressionist exhibition.

Maximilien Luce, *Georges Seurat,* 1891.

While Seurat admired plein-air painting and the Impressionists' bright colors, he wanted to make forms more solid and "deepen the (canvas) surface." He achieved this by using small dots of contrasting and pure color to reduce form to its basic geometric shape. The result is that his paintings have a "frozen" look, a sharp contrast to the fleeting effects the Impressionists sought. Seurat's new scientific approach was called **pointillism.**

> **Pointillism** is placing little dots of pure color next to each other so that, from a distance, a viewer's eye will mix them into an even brighter color. This technique is also called **divisionism,** the term that Seurat preferred to use.

Georges Pierre Seurat

Georges Seurat, *A Sunday on the Grande Jatte,* 1884–1886. The Grande Jatte, or big jetty, is an island in the Seine River near Paris.

A Closer Look

- Notice the 1886-style big bustle "pouf" on dresses.
- Look for animals (monkey and dogs) and sports (rowing and fishing). Notice how figures get smaller as they recede into space.
- Seurat often frames his paintings with a border of dots.
- What kinds of activities do you find in a park today?

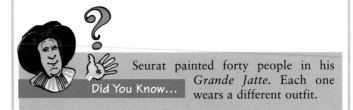

Did You Know... Seurat painted forty people in his *Grande Jatte.* Each one wears a different outfit.

Color findings in a tapestry factory While working in a tapestry factory, chemist Eugene Chevreul studied color. His findings, published in 1839, influenced the Impressionists and Post Impressionists—particularly Seurat. Chevreul noticed that strands of different colored wool placed next to each other affected how the other looked. He observed that the eye blends two adjoining colors into one. This is called *optical mixing*. If yellow and blue are next to each other, the eye will blend them into green. Chevreul also noticed that a color standing alone is surrounded by a faint halo of its complementary color.

ART S COOP

Protesting pointillism When Seurat entered *Grande Jatte* in the last Impressionist Exhibition of 1886, Monet, Sisley, and Renoir took their paintings out of the show in protest. They objected to Seurat's labored and scientific approach to art.

Why did Seurat make so few paintings? Seurat died young, at age thirty-two. Some of his larger works took many months to paint. *Grande Jatte* was sixty-seven square feet and took him more than a year to finish. He needed a ladder to reach the top. Placing same-sized dots next to each other was a slow process.

Curtain Call

The presence of Seurat's *La Grande Jatte* in the last Impressionist exhibition signaled the break up of Impressionism. The new pointillist style brought outdoor painting back inside the studio, away from the natural world of changing light effects important to the Impressionists. Seurat's new approach to painting opened the way to a variety of new styles in the twentieth century.

Georges Pierre Seurat

Georges Seurat, *Eiffel Tower,* circa 1889.

A Closer Look

Using Seurat's ideas about line and color, what do you think he thought about the new Eiffel Tower? His upward curves and warm happy colors suggest he liked it. How do you think Seurat would have painted the Statue of Liberty?

Georges Pierre Seurat

An eyeful! Designed by Gustave Eiffel, the Eiffel Tower was built for the 1889 World's Fair in Paris. It was the tallest structure in the world. It was supposed to come down in 1909 but was saved because its antenna was important to French radio broadcasts. Pissarro also painted the 984-foot tower.

Did You Know...

Eiffel Tower, Paris. **You** are one of the first people to see this photograph. It has never been published before!

Seeing blue Seurat had a theory that color and line change our moods. He said that dark, cold colors are sad. Light tones and warm colors are cheerful. Upturned lines are happy; downward ones are gloomy.

Paintmate **Camille Pissarro** was looking for a greater depth in his art, and tried Seurat's pointillist technique for about four years. Seurat was happy that an older and better-known artist supported him. Some art critics could not always tell their paintings apart!

Activities

Hunts

Hiking hunt Look for the size of canvas you would pretend to carry to paint plein-air. Next hunt for a landscape where you would set up your easel. While standing in the gallery, sketch the landscape.

Brushstroke hunt Count the different kinds of brushstrokes in one painting without getting too close to the canvas. Compare the number you get with a friend.

Paint hunt Find examples of globs, dollops, dots, commas, squiggles, slashes, sticks, points, and strokes of paint.

Signature hunt Try to find a signature by Cézanne or van Gogh. They are very rare. What is the most popular place for artists to sign their work?

Japanese woodblock print hunt Compare the color and composition with Impressionist paintings.

"Just don't like it" hunt Find a painting that you don't like. Stare at it and try to find one good thing in it. A color, shape, the frame, the story. Have a friend do the same thing and compare notes.

Games and Activities

Elbow room Each player chooses a painting in a gallery, then applies the **ELBOW** mnemonic (page 24).

Five questions Gather three people. One person chooses a painting and keeps it a secret. Each person may ask five questions to figure out the secret painting. Questions are answered with a **yes** or **no.** The person who guesses the painting wins and chooses the next painting.

Create your own composition Find an open door or window. Look through it. What is closest to you? What is farthest away? What is in between? Notice the colors. Cool greens, blues, and whites? The warm pinks of a sunrise or sunset? Look for straight lines of trees on a calm day or the diagonal, bending trees of a windy day. Notice the parallel lines of tall or low buildings. Do lines converge on roads to form shapes like triangles? Arrange the view through your window or door in the same way you would line up a camera shot. When it is just right for your eye, you have completed a composition.

That's *my* birthday! Is your birthday or someone else's you know in the following list of dates? Turn to page 74 to find out which artist has your birthday.

Turn to page 74 to find out which artist has your birthday.

> January 14, 19, 25
> February 14, 25
> March 30
> May 22
> June 7
> July 10, 19
> October 30
> December 2

Art Works

Fill the frame When you have found a painting in your gallery by one of the Impressionists, write the title under the artist's frame. Then draw something from the painting in the artist's frame.

Create a "Seurat mosaic" Collect eight pieces of primary and complementary color construction paper. Glue tiny pieces of each color to make a picture. You may want to sketch first.

Recreate a painting Find an Impressionist painting that has some kind of transportation in it. Copy it but replace the transportation with 21st century transport.

Recreate your favorite painting at home. Use short strokes to sketch your favorite painting.

Plein air painting Take paper and crayons outside. Find something that the sun has hit which has a shadow. Draw the object while paying attention to the shape and color of its shadow.

Writing

Weekend away Find a landscape or group of people you would like to visit. Write about how the landscape and the people looked and how they affected you.

Throwback Look at a magazine and find a photo you like. How would it look if an Impressionist had painted it?

Prose to poetry Read a biography of an artist in an encyclopedia. Put the information in a poem. Use the letters of his or her name to give you structure:

> **M** illions
> **O** f dabs
> **N** ow create
> **E** nchanted
> **T** ime

Personality paint Find a portrait of a person and study it. Create a story about his or her personality. Use at least one color to describe the person's character or mood. Think of van Gogh.

Recipes

Pêche Melba (Peach Melba)

When the Impressionists were painting, opera was popular in Paris. French chefs liked to create dishes to honor the famous opera singers. In 1894 the French chef Auguste Escoffier created a peach dessert for Nellie Melba, an Australian opera star. It is called Peach Melba and is one of the best-known "opera" recipes.

Peel and halve fresh peaches. Place them on vanilla ice cream. Puree fresh or frozen raspberries and sweeten with confectioners' sugar. Pour over peaches and ice cream.

Monet's Tarte Tatin (Caramel-Apple Pie)

Monet sometimes drove several hours to eat his favorite Tarte Tatin. Its real name is Tarte des Demoiselles Tatin (tart of the Tatin girls). Legend says that Caroline and Stephanie Tatin ran an inn. The menu featured their father's favorite caramel topped apple pie. One day the dessert fell upside down from its pan and a classic French dessert was born!

Butter a 9-inch baking dish 2½ inches deep. Add a layer of fine sugar ⅓ inch thick. Cover with peeled and quartered apples. Add dots of butter and more sugar to the top.

For crust:
3¾ cup sifted flour
1¼ cups soft butter
1 egg
½–¾ cup water
5 tbs. of fine sugar
1½ tsp. of salt

Blend all the ingredients except the flour together. Gradually add the flour until you have a dough. Chill the mixture and roll it out. Place on top of the apples. Bake at 375° for 25–30 minutes. Serve upside down and hot.

Seurat Tart

Seurat did not eat this tart, but you will see why it is named for him when you make it. Red and blue berries are placed on the crust just as he painted dots of color on his canvas.

1 cup blueberries
1 cup raspberries
¼ cup sugar

Pie crust:
1½ sticks butter
1¼ cups flour
½ cup sugar
½ tsp. baking powder
pinch of salt

Mix and bake the pie crust in a 9-inch pan for 15 minutes at 350°. Remove and sprinkle berries and sugar on the crust. Return to oven for 20 more minutes at 375°. Serve with whipped cream.

Artists' Birthdays

January
14th   Berthe Morisot
19th   Paul Cézanne
25th   Edouard Manet

February
14th   Claude Monet
25th   Pierre-Auguste Renoir

March
30th   Vincent van Gogh

May
22nd   Mary Cassatt

June
7th   Paul Gauguin

July
10th   Camille Pissarro
19th   Edgar Degas

October
30th   Alfred Sisley

December
2nd   Georges Pierre Seurat

Were *you* born on the same day as one of the artists in this book? Check here and find out!

Credits

cover Pierre Auguste Renoir, *Luncheon of the Boating Party*, 1881. Oil on canvas, 51 x 68 in (129.5 x 172.7 cm). The Phillips Collection, Washington, DC.

PAGE

2 Rembrandt (Rembrandt Harmensz. van Rijn), *Artist in His Studio*, ca. 1629. Oil on panel, 9¾ x 12½ in (24.8 x 31.7 cm). Zoe Oliver Sherman Collection. Given in memory of Lillie Oliver Poor. Courtesy Museum of Fine Arts, Boston.

7 Alfred Sisley, *Bougival*, 1876. Oil on canvas. Cincinnati Art Museum, The John J. Emery Fund 1922.38.

9 Pierre Auguste Renoir, *Woman with Parasol and a Small Child on a Sunlit Hillside*. Oil on canvas, 18½ x 22⅛ in (47 x 56.2 cm). Bequest of John T. Spaulding, Courtesy Museum of Fine Arts, Boston.

9 Jacques Henri Lartigue, *Cousin Caro and Mr. Plantevigne, Villerville*, 1906. Photograph by Jacques Henri Lartigue. © Ministère de la Culture-France/A.A.J.H.L.

10 Jan van Huysum, *Vase of Flowers*, c. 1720. Oil on panel, 31 x 23⅓ in (79 x 60 cm). ©Nelson-Atkins Musuem of Art, Kansas City, Missouri.

11 *Red-eyed tree frog.* Courtesy Tony Stone Images, Chicago, Illinois.

11 Pablo Picasso, *Woman Seated in a Chair*, 1941. Oil on canvas, 51 x 38 in (131 x 97.6 cm). The Currier Gallery of Art, Anonymous gift, 1953.3.

12 Edouard Manet, *Boating*, 1874. Oil on canvas, 38¼ x 51¼ in (97.2 x 130.2 cm). Photograph ©1994 The Metropolitan Museum of Art, H.O. Havemeyer Collection, Bequest of Mrs. H.O. Havemeyer, 1929. (29.100.115).

13 Pierre Auguste Renoir, *Dance at Bougival*, 1883. Oil on canvas, 71⅞ x 38⅝ in (181.8 x 98.1 cm). Picture Fund. Courtesy the Museum of Fine Arts, Boston.

14 Paul Cézanne, *Mont Sainte Victoire seen from the Bibemus Quarry*, c. 1897. Oil on canvas, 25⅓ x 31⅓ in (65.1 x 80 cm). The Baltimore Museum of Art: The Cone Collection, formed by Dr. Claribel Cone and Miss Etta Cone of Baltimore, Maryland. BMA 1950.196

15 *African Road.* Photograph courtesy W. Knapp.

16 *Policeman: "Lady, it would be unwise to enter!"* Cartoon from Le Charivari.

17 Edouard Manet, *A Café Interior*, 1869. Pen and black ink on pale tan wove paper, darkened to reddish-brown, 11½ x 15⅝ in (29.5 x 39.5 cm). Courtesy of the Fogg Art Museum, Harvard University Art Museums, Bequest of Meta and Paul J. Sachs.

19 Claude Monet, *Impression: Sunrise*, 1872. Oil on canvas, 18½ x 24½ in (48 x 63 cm). Courtesy the Musée Marmottan-Claude Monet and Giraudon, Paris.

20 William Bouguereau, *Homer and His Guide*, 1874. Oil on canvas, 82¼ x 56¼ in (2.11 x 1.44 m). Layton Art Collection, Milwaukee Art Museum, Gift of Frederick Layton.

21 Winslow Homer, *Copyists in the Louvre Gallery, Paris,* 1868 from *Harper's Weekly* 12 (11 January 1868), p. 25. Wood engraving, 9¹⁄₁₆ x 13¹¹⁄₁₆ in (23.2 x 35.8 cm). Photograph © Addison Gallery of American Art, Phillips Academy, Andover, MA. All rights reserved.

22 Félicien Myrbach-Rheinfeld, *Candidates for admission to the Paris Salon,* ca. 1885. Courtesy The Metropolitan Museum of Art, Harris Brisbane Dick Fund, 1947. (47.53.19).

22 *The Terrible Jury.* Courtesy the Bibliothèque Nationale, Paris.

23 *The Salon of 1879—The Preview.* Drawing by Maurice Leloir. Photograph courtesy the Bibliothèque Nationale, Paris.

26 *Manet by Nadar.* Photograph courtesy the Bibliothèque Nationale, Paris.

26 *Courtyard, Louvre Museum.* Photograph courtesy Suzanne Terry.

27. Edouard Manet, *Le Déjeuner sur l'herbe (Luncheon on the Grass),* 1863. Oil on canvas, 7 ft x 8 ft 10 in (2.15 x 2.72 m). Musée d'Orsay, Paris. ©Photo RMN.

28 Marcantonio Raimondi, *The Judgment of Paris* (detail). Engraving, 11⅝ x 17³⁄₁₆ in (29.8 x 44.4 cm). Yale University Art Gallery, Gift of Edward B. Greene, Yale 1900.

29 *Manet's* Wintergarden *hanging in a German salt mine.* Photograph courtesy the National Archives and Records Adminstration, Washington, DC.

30 *Berthe Morisot by Pierre Petit,* 1869. Rouart Collection. Photograph courtesy Jean -Loup Charmet, Paris.

31 Berthe Morisot, *In the Dining Room,* 1886. Oil on canvas, 24⅛ x 19¾ in (61 x 50 cm). Chester Dale Collection, © 1997 Board of Trustees, National Gallery of Art, Washington.

32 *Portrait of Degas by Barnes.* Photograph courtesy the Bibliothèque Nationale, Paris.

33 Edgas Degas, *Waiting: Dancer and Woman with Umbrella on a Bench (L'Attente),* c. 1882. Pastel on paper, 19 x 24 in (48.2 x 61 cm). Owned jointly with the Norton Simon Art Foundation, Pasadena. The J. Paul Getty Museum, Los Angeles.

34 Edgar Degas, *The Little Dancer of Fourteen Years,* no. 45. Bronze, H: 39 in (100.2 cm). © Sterling and Francine Clark Art Institute, Williamstown, Massachusetts. Photograph © 1994 Clark Art Institute, Williamstown, MA.

35 George Eastman, *Mr. Nadar, Place de l'Opéra, Paris.* Kodak Snapshot #2. Photograph courtesy George Eastman House, Rochester, NY.

36 Edgar Degas, M. and Mme. Edouard Manet, c. 1868-69. Oil on canvas, 25⅝ x 28 in (65.8 x 72 cm). Kitakyushu Municipal Museum of Art (0-119).

38 *Madam Joseph Durand-Ruel, Mary Cassatt, an unidentified friend, and Marie-Louise Durand-Ruel at Mesnil-Theribus, September 1910, photographed by Joseph Durand-Ruel.* Photograph courtesy Durand-Ruel and Company, Paris. Document Archives Durand-Ruel.

39 Mary Cassatt, *Mother and Child,* c. 1890. Oil on canvas, 35⅜ x 25⅜ in (91 x 65.2 cm). The Roland P. Murdock Collection, Wichita Art Museum, Wichita, Kansas.

40 Totoya Hokkei, *The Jewel That Shines at Night,* early 1830s. Ink on paper. Mead Art Museum, Gift of William Green 1990.36.

41 Pierre August Renoir, *Monet Painting in his Garden at Argenteuil,* 1873. Oil on canvas. Bequest of Anne Parrish Titzell 1957.614, © Wadsworth Atheneum.

42 *Camille Pissarro with Julie, Paul-Emile, and Jeanne in the Orchard at Eragny.* Reserved to the Ashmolean Museum, Oxford.

43 Camille Pissarro, *Haying Time,* 1892. Oil on canvas, 25½ x 31⅔ in

(65.5 x 81.3 cm). Helen Birch Bartlett Memorial Collection, 1926.252.
Photograph ©1997, The Art Institute of Chicago, All Rights Reserved.
46 *Claude Monet photographed by Sardnal,* 1897. Photograph courtesy
Durand-Ruel and Company, Paris. All rights reserved—Document
Archives Durand-Ruel, Paris.
47 Claude Monet, *Haystacks,* 1889. Oil on canvas, 25½ x 36¼ in (65.5 x
93.2 cm). Hill-Stead Museum, Farmington, Connecticut.
49 Claude Monet, *The Gare Saint-Lazare: Arrival of a Train,* 1877. Oil
on canvas, 31⅝ x 38⅝ in (81.2 x 99.2 cm). Courtesy of the Fogg Art
Museum, Harvard University Art Museums, Bequest from the Collection
of Maurice Wertheim, Class of 1906.
50 *Sisley by Ramsay.* Photograph courtesy the Bibliothèque Nationale,
Paris.
51 Alfred Sisley, *Bougival,* 1876. Oil on canvas. Cincinnati Art Museum,
The John J. Emery Fund 1922.38.
52 *Renoir seated in his studio,* c. 1912. Photograph courtesy Durand-Ruel
and Company, Paris. All rights reserved - Document Archives Durand-
Ruel.
53 Pierre Auguste Renoir, *Luncheon of the Boating Party,* 1881. Oil on
canvas, 51 x 68 in (129.5 x 172.7 cm). The Phillips Collection,
Washington, DC.
54 Pierre Auguste Renoir, *Les Grands Boulevards,* 1875. Oil on canvas,
20½ x 25 in (52.7 x 64.3 cm). Philadelphia Museum of Art: The Henry P.
McIlhenny Collection in memory of Frances P. McIlhenny 1986.26-29.
55 Paul Cézanne, *Self-Portrait with a Beret,* c. 1898-99. Oil on canvas,
25¼ x 21 in (64 x 53.5 cm). Charles H. Bayley Picture and Painting Fund,
and partial Gift of Elizabeth Paine Metcalf, Courtesy the Museum of Fine
Arts, Boston.
56 Paul Cézanne, *Basket of Apples,* c. 1895. Oil on canvas, 25½ x 31⅔ in
(65.5 x 81.3 cm). Helen Birch Bartlett Memorial Collection, 1926.252.
Photograph ©1997, The Art Institute of Chicago, All Rights Reserved.
59 *Gauguin in Oceania.* Photograph courtesy the Bibliothèque Nationale,
Paris.
60 Paul Gauguin, *Vahine No Te Vi (Woman of the Mango),* 1892. Oil on
canvas, 28¼ x 17⅓ in (72.7 x 44.5 cm). The Baltimore Museum of Art:
The Cone Collection, formed by Dr. Claribel Cone and Miss Etta Cone of
Baltimore, Maryland, BMA 1950.213.
63 Vincent van Gogh, *Self-Potrait Dedicated to Paul Gauguin,* 1888. Oil
on canvas, 23¼ x 19 in (59.75 x 48.83 cm). Courtesy of the Fogg Art
Museum, Harvard University Art Museums, Bequest from the Collection
of Maurice Wertheim, Class of 1906. © President and Fellows Harvard
College, Harvard University Art Museums.
62 Vincent van Gogh, *Bedroom at Arles,* 1888. Oil on canvas, 28½ x 36 in
(73.6 x 92.3 cm). Helen Birch Bartlett Memorial Collection, 1926.417.
Photograph ©1995, The Art Institute of Chicago, All Rights Reserved.
65   Maximilien Luce, *Georges Seurat.* Photograph courtesy the
Bibliothèque Nationale, Paris.
66 Georges Seurat, *A Sunday on La Grande Jatte,* 1884. Oil on canvas,
80¾ x 119⅗ in (207.5 x 308 cm). Helen Birch Bartlett Memorial
Collection, 1926.224. Photograph ©1997, The Art Institute of Chicago.
All Rights Reserved.
68 Georges Seurat, *Eiffel Tower,* c. 1889. Oil on panel, 9½ x 6 in (24 x
15 cm). Fine Arts Museum of San Francisco, Museum purchase, William
H. Noble Bequest Fund, 1979.48.
69 *Eiffel Tower, Paris, Snap shot #2.* Photograph courtesy George
Eastman House, Rochester, NY.

Index